CHORUS OF CICADAS

Exploring the Ecology, Biology, and Cultural Significance of Nature's Singing Insects

By

Kathleen Haly

1

Table Of Contents

Introduction
  Importance of Cicadas in Ecosystems

Chapter 1: The Life Cycle of Cicadas
  Egg Stage
  Nymph Stage
  Adult Stage

Chapter 2: Types of Cicadas
  Annual Cicadas
  Periodical Cicadas

Chapter 3: Distribution and Habitat
  Global Distribution
  Preferred Habitats

Chapter 4: Cicada's Behaviors
  Reproduction
  Cicadas Communication
  Feeding Habits

Chapter 5: The Role of Cicadas in Nature

  Ecological Importance

  Cicadas Interactions with Other Species

Chapter 6: Cicadas in Culture and Folklore

  Historical References

  Cultural Significances

Conclusion

Introduction

The insects known as cicadas, colloquially entitled "the heralds of summer," are among the most intriguing creatures in the order Hemiptera and fall into the family Cicadidae. They have more than 3,000 species across the world and they are famous because of their distinctive sounds that are produced by males for attracting females during mating.

To begin with, it is well-known that cicadas possess a peculiar life cycle which could take several years to complete. The majority of them have a three-step life cycle comprising egg-nymph-adults. Female ones lay eggs into plant stems which hatch into nymphs. These nymphs then subsequently dig beneath the ground where they feed on plant roots' sap for many years depending on species. After accomplishing their development, adults – still called nymphs – emerge from the soil while shedding their exoskeletons with them; later they die within a few weeks or months after laying eggs.

Their diversity in size, color and song patterns is one of the most distinctive characteristics of cicadas. While some are small and only a few centimeters long, others can grow up to several inches. Moreover, their colors vary considerably from dull shades of brown and green to bright ones like red, yellow or blue with wings sometimes adorned with intricate designs. Each species of cicada has its own specialized song that is produced by structures called tymbals located on the abdomen of the male individuals. These songs function as a communication tool among individuals and are also important for finding mates.

Cicadas are important as well as beautiful in several ecosystems globally. As a herbivore, nymphs and adults eat tree sap and other plant fluids which may have positive or negative impacts on their hosts. While overfeeding by young cicadas can harm small trees and shrubs, it contributes to recycling of nutrients and soil aeration. This way, the condition of all the forests' health is improved. Also, cicadas are vital to the survival of many predators including birds, mammals such as monkeys and reptiles. Others are bugs that feed on other insects.

Moreover, cicadas hold cultural or symbolic values in different societies. In various parts of this world there were cultures where cicadas were highly respected, being viewed as a representation for rebirth, eternal life and transformation in some cases. After years of hibernation they come out from beneath the ground implying fresh starts again; hence folklores, myths, literature and poetry revolving around them becomes so captivating until the present day. Moreover their songs function as artistry stimulation sounds that inspire artists across time.

Besides their ecological significance cicadas have rich cultural symbolic importance in many communities. In different places around the globe like Asia pacific countries have recognized them as symbols associated with immortality resurrection or change of some kind particularly rebirth after long periods of hiding underground which are usually accompanied by rejuvenation and revival making these creatures very fascinating subjects in mythology legends stories books etc about them All along ages they also inspired musicians poets creators alike due to recurring bug sounds.

Importance of Cicadas in Ecosystems

Cicadas are very important in the ecosystem as they contribute to various ecological processes and food webs. Their significance, therefore, emanates from their nymphing and adulting as well as interacting with other organisms that reside in their habitats.

Among the most significant ecological roles cicadas play is being herbivorous. While still underground, during this time as a nymph, Cicada larvae suck sap from plant roots for years depending on the species' type of Cicada. Although there are instances when excessive feeding by nymphs can hurt young trees and shrubs, this also helps in promoting nutrient cycling and soil aeration. In this regard, cicadas contribute to organic matter decomposition through root pruning and excretion of waste products thus enriching the soil with nutrients necessary for the overall health of forest ecosystems.

Moreover, cicadas are a critical food source for several predators such as birds, reptiles, mammals and other insects. Predators heavily rely on them because of the availability and regularity that arise during mass emergences like brood years. Furthermore, predation of cicadas helps to control their population sizes and maintain ecosystem balance. Additionally, when they decompose their corpses, nutrients are recycled while scavengers and decomposers have some more feeding materials.

Cicadas also play a role in altering the dynamics of ecosystems through the way they interact with other living things. For example, the rhythmic sound of cicada songs can attract predators and parasitoids thereby resulting in increase pressure of predation on other insects populations. Similarly, when immature stages of these insects are present roots may be pruned as well as nutrient cycling may take place that can affect species composition and diversity among plant communities.

Generally speaking, cicada's importance goes beyond individual biology to include how they relate with other organisms in an ecosystem and their contribution to processes in it. Understanding these fascinating animals is vital for sustaining healthy natural ecosystems worldwide as well as conserving them.

Chapter 1: The Life Cycle of Cicadas

Egg Stage

The egg stage represents the first part of their life cycle, and from that phase eggs develop into adult cicadas. At this critical phase, female cicadas lay eggs on suitable substrates such as plant tissues or soil in which they grow until they hatch to nymphs.

The females of some species possess modified ovipositors for embedding eggs into different substrates. They may insert them into the stems, twigs or branches or over the soil in small openings depending on the kind of the cicada. The choice of site is determined by various factors including species specificity, environmental determinants/conditions and substrate availability.

Cicada eggs are left alone for incubation where they develop and grow into embryos after deposition. The length of time an egg takes before hatching varies among different cicada species with some lasting weeks while others several months depending on temperature, humidity and life history traits.

The eggs are subject to predation, parasitism and environmental stressors during incubation. Like having oviposition places hidden, selecting healthy host plants, or laying many eggs to compensate for losses.

At the end of the incubation period, egg undergoes some physiological changes in anticipation of hatching. Such changes can entail formation of specialized structures like respiratory appendages that enhance gaseous exchange and respiration within it.

Eggs at maturity hatch producing nymphs called nymphal hatchlings or first instar nymphs. These newly hatched nymphs emerge from the eggshells and start their journey underground where they will spend most of their lives feeding on plant roots and molting several times before becoming adults.

The egg stage is arguably one of the most vital phases in a cicada's life cycle, as it sets precedence for subsequent developmental stages and ultimately contributes to perpetuating populations of cicadas themselves. Knowledge about factors affecting egg deposition, incubation and hatching is necessary for understanding ecological dynamics of cicada population as well as its interactions with the environment where it occurs.

Cicada life cycle begins with egg stage where, eggs are laid, incubated and nymph is born. This period is important for understanding population dynamics and ecological relationships among cicadas; therefore a more detailed study of this phase is highly encouraged.

Nymph Stage

The climax of the cicada life cycle occurs in the nymph stage, which follows egg hatching and ends with maturity. After being hatched from eggs, female cicadas diversify into several stages on their way to become fully grown adults.

Cicadas spend their nymphal stage underground where they use piercing-sucking mouthparts to feed on plant root sap. This subterranean lifestyle can last for many years depending on the species; some cicada species have long-lived nymphs that can take up to a decade to complete development. At this time, the nymphs molt as they grow and develop by shedding off their exoskeletons.

Each instar phase is associated with unique physiological and morphological changes. When molting takes place, the old cuticles are discarded: larger and more developed bodies appear. This phenomenon known as ecdysis allows for growth during subsequent instars until attainment of maturity.

The nymph stage is a very important period for cicadas, during which they assimilate the necessary resources and energy to undergo transformation into adults. Nymphs must navigate beneath the soil, find suitable food sources and elude predators as well as any other environmental threats that may come their way until they reach adulthood.

When the nymphs are almost fully developed, they have their final molt and shed off their exoskeletons in their nymphal form. This emergence process, referred to as mass emergence or "cicada emergence", involves synchronized bursts which often cause great attention due to large numbers of cicadas involved.

The nymph stage is an integral part of a life cycle of a cicada where it resides undergound, molts many times while accumulating resources for its metamorphosis into an adult. This stage is critical in shaping cicada populations and their ecological relationships thus emphasizing the need for further study on nymphal development specifically.

Adult Stage

The adulative level of cicadas is the apex of their incredible life cycle, and it is also marked by the advent of winged adults from underground nymphal chambers. It is a stage marked by a limited but very intense period of activity within which they mate, lay eggs and contribute to ecological dynamics in their environment.

Once out of the ground, adult cicadas undergo a process called eclosion where the last nymphal exoskeleton is shed and wings expanded to full size. At first , they are soft and vulnerable but soon harden and darken as the exoskeletons sclerotize, giving support for flight and other activities.

Compared to their elongated nymphal development period which can be up to several years for some species, adult cicadas have rather short lives that may span from few weeks to few months depending on a given species. During this time, their main purpose becomes reproduction so as to ensure perpetuation of the next generation of cicadas.

The production of loud, buzzing calls by adult cicadas is one of the most conspicuous behaviors that can be attributed to them, especially males who are seeking mates. The tymbals found in the abdomen produce these sounds and they serve as a way to communicate as well as determining success of breeding.

Once mating has taken place, female cicadas insert eggs into suitable plant tissues such as twigs or branches using their ovipositors. Each female is capable of laying hundreds of eggs that will hatch into nymphs to perpetuate the life cycle for another generation of cicadas.

Apart from reproduction activities, adult cicadas also play a significant role in ecosystem functioning. They can affect the health and vigor of host plants because they feed on plant fluids by means of piercing-sucking mouthparts. Additionally, adult cicadas become food sources to different predators like birds, mammals and other insects hence promoting trophic dynamics within ecosystems.

Ultimately, when adults become fully grown after molting their skins for about five years or more it is a critical stage in their life cycle where they perform reproductive duties and participate in ecological processes within their environment before dying from natural causes.

Chapter 2: Types of Cicadas

Annual Cicadas

The annual cicadas, which are known as dog day cicadas, are an interesting group of insects belonging to the genus Tibicen and mostly found in North America. Annual cicadas have a shorter life cycle than their periodical counterparts, developing within one or several years rather than emerging all at once every 13 or 17 years. Such variations make them fascinating creatures for scientific observation and inquiry by both entomologists and lovers of nature.

Annual cicada's relatively short life span is one of the differences they possess from those of periodical cicadas. Nymphs spend most time underground while the periodical cicadas emerge in mass-broods that coincide with each other; on the other hand, adults show up either summer or toward end of season

The buzzing calls of annual cicadas can be heard in many places during sweltering summer days. Primarily emitted by males to attract mates, these calls are usually loud and continuous hence becoming a distinguishing point for people living in areas where there are high numbers of annual cicadas during summer chorus.

Annual cicadas are important and have many ecological roles. They suck plant fluids with their piercing-sucking mouthparts as they develop into adults (not only this) that can also affect the host plants' health and strength. Feeding behavior at times damages trees and shrubs while still playing a part in recycling nutrients among other ecosystem dynamics.

The nymphs of annual cicadas live underground for several years, living on sap from plant roots and shedding their exoskeletons during growth and development. This long period of life under the soil helps them to establish contact with host plants and form strong relationships with particular species of trees.

At last, after spending several years underground nymphs come out as grown-ups leaving behind their old outer skins to spread wings for flight. Large adult cicadas develop from nymphs by discarding their exoskeleton to become winged insects. They are easily distinguishable from others due to their (big size/full bodies/robust abdomens/massive thoraxes/huge eyes/eyes that stick out).

The mating ritual of annual cicadas involves a show where males croak loudly to call females. After mating, the female uses her ovipositors to place eggs at favorable locations, like twigs or branches. Each female lays hundreds of eggs that guarantee progeny survival for next season's cicadas.

Annual cicadas play a critical role in the ecosystem towards nutrient cycling, plant vitality and food chain. Their characteristic sounds, unique life cycle and environmental roles make them a captivating study and an object of admiration to any nature lover.

Periodical Cicadas

Among the world's most baffling and puzzling insects are the periodical cicadas, members of the genus Magicicada. These remarkable creatures are famous for their synchronized emergence: they appear in large numbers every 13 or 17 years in specific broods all over North America. The phenomenon of periodical cicadas has held in awe scientists, entomologists and the public for centuries, resulting into extensive research as well as appreciation for their glorious biology and behavior.

Periodical cicadas have one of nature's most amazing life cycles. Unlike annual cicadas that emerge yearly, these periodic ones spend the majority of their lives underground as nymphs feasting on sap from tree roots. These nymphs stay dormant either for 13 or 17 years depending on the species and brood going through molts and growth stages before they eventually come out.

The synchronous emergence of periodical cicadas is a spectacle unequaled in any other insect group. Billions of cicada nymphs bore en masse to the surface when soil temperature hits a certain threshold which usually occurs late spring or early summer. By overwhelming predators with their sheer numbers and increasing chances of successful reproduction, this synchronization guarantees high survival rates for the species.

Periodical cicadas are categorized into distinct broods, each with its own emerging time-table and geographical distribution. These are referred to as broods where they are numbered using roman numerals so that they can be easily identified based on the range of their emergence and the specific gap between successive emergence or the duration of their emergence. Examples include Brood X (10) and Brood XIII (13), which represent different American regions having well-known periodical cicada broods.

The deafening chorus of male periodical cicadas is a defining feature of their emergence. Males make loud unique sounds like buzzing or clicking to attract females during mating. In densely populated areas, thousands of males' cacophony through these quiet sounds at once.

After mating, females lay eggs in tree branches using their ovipositors—it protects them from predators and environmental factors. After dying off within a few weeks, adult cicadas leave behind a new generation of eggs that will hatch and start hundreds more years of breeding and hatching before restarting this cycle over again.

Periodical cicadas have a massive and multi-faceted ecological impact. This is because their coming out of the ground provides an extensive food source for various predators, including birds, mammals and insects that devour the plentiful crop of cicadas. Moreover, the bodies of these insects are highly nutritious thus contributing to soil fertility and ecosystem wellbeing through enrichment of plants thereby leading to better plant growth and development.

Additionally, periodical cicadas play a major role in forest ecology by promoting biodiversity and affecting tree physiology. Female oviposition may sometimes result in damage to different branches of trees; although this damage is generally minimal it does not pose major threats to the tree's health. Instead, regular occurrence of cicadas leads to accelerated tree growth rates as well as nutrient cycling that ultimately enhances overall forest ecosystem health.

Periodic cicada is an amazing insect with a unique life cycle and ecological importance. Their synchronous emergencies hold our attention and really make us want to witness them directly. Through their fascinating biology and behavior, periodic cicadas have earned their place in nature as one of its special creatures which never cease captivating scientists in addition to those who are interested in nature.

Chapter 3: Distribution and Habitat

Global Distribution

Cicadas, an assortment of insects under the Hemiptera order, inhabit every continent except Antarctica. Its worldwide incursion is very great and diverse in terms of niche from tropical forests to arid deserts and mountainous ecosystems to temperate woodlands. Although some species are more prevalent in certain regions of the world, cicadas have acclimatized themselves into nearly all climates and ecosystems globally indicating their extreme resilience and adaptability.

In areas like South America, Africa as well as Southeast Asia which are characterized by rainforests and hot savannas; these cicadas are found. Here the highest number of species for cicada occur here with numerous species occupying different niches within various ecosystems. For example, in Amazon Rainforest the sounds created by this insect along with others create a loud noise that fills up air where they play significant roles in pollination process, nutrient cycling as well as food webs.

The moderate regions in the world, which include North America, Europe and parts of Asia are as well home to a great variety of cicada species. In these places, these insects are more active during the hot seasons where they come out from under the ground and make love on trees and shrubs. The United States has common annual cicadas that are found all over but living in different areas with various species occupying various locations starting from deciduous forests to urban regions. The periodic emergence of periodical cicadas in North America is a particularly notable phenomenon, attracting attention from scientists and the public alike.

Also present therein are kinds of cicadas adapted for such desert environments like Australian Outback and Southwest US. Such cicadas' distinctive feature is adaptation to surviving in harsh desert conditions: they have evolved physiological changes specific for this region that allows them to hide underground when it becomes too hot or reduce their activities during the hottest hours of the day so as not to lose water through perspiration.

It is even true that cicadas in mountainous regions, like the Himalayas, Andes and Rocky Mountains have come to adapt to the high altitude environment. These cicadas are more tolerant of cold weather and thin air, and they often inhabit alpine meadows and montane forests. Within such habitats, cicadas have important roles in ecosystems where they take part in nutrient cycles as well as serve as food for a number of predators including some birds and mammals.

The distribution of cicadas is influenced by several factors such as climate, habitat availability and presence of suitable host plants. Some species may have narrow ranges only occurring in certain microhabitats while others are generalist which means that they can adjust to a wider range of environmental conditions. Additionally, human activities like deforestation, urbanization and climate change also affect populations of cicadas leading to various distributions thus making it difficult for their conservation or management.

Cicadas exist everywhere on earth, wherever it is a continent and global ecosystem that has several continents. No matter whether there are tropical rain forests or dry deserts, northern forest or mountains cicadas play are instrumental in the health of ecosystems worldwide leading to biodiversity, functioning of the ecosystem and intricate web of life on the planet Earth. It is important for conservation purposes and also to appreciate the incredible insect diversity in our world when considering cicadas' global distribution.

Preferred Habitats

Cicadas are captivating insects that have diverse preferences for where they live, indicating that they can survive in different environmental conditions. Though different species may have dissimilar habitat needs, there are certain common traits that mark preferred cicada habitats across varied regions and ecosystems.

1. Trees and shrubs: Often associated with vegetation, particularly trees and shrubs, Cicadas lay eggs on these plants and feed on sap from them. Many cicada species prefer deciduous forests featuring several tree types. For instance, Magicicada cicadas like hardwood trees like oak, hickory or maple. In tropical zones where vegetation is luxuriantly rich, cicadas reside in numerous tree species within rainforests or savannahs.

2. Water supply: This means that areas with water sources suitable for their sustenance and growth are more likely to host cicadas than

33

others without such resources. In wet tropical environments such as rainforests and swamps, moisture abundance results in flourishing of the insect group called cicada. However even in arid zones they can be found around water bodies such as rivers, streams etc due to better vegetation hence increased accessibility to water.

3. Temperature: Cicada's selection of habitat is mostly dependent on the temperature since this affects their seasonality and activity patterns. Some species are adapted to living in tropical regions that are warm throughout the year while some others inhabit temperate zones which have four distinct seasons. The cicadas in these regions emerge in summer months when temperatures are most favorable for mating and egg laying.

4. Soil Type: Soil type also plays a significant role in determining the habitat preferences of cicadas especially during the nymphal stage where they live underground. Nymphs prefer well-drained soils because too much moisture can kill them. For burrowing, sandy or loamy soils are highly favored as nymphs bore into them and feed on root sap without worrying about drowning.

5. Altitude: Certain cicadas can be found at lowland altitudes, while others occur at higher altitudes within montane regions. These include mountainous regions with cooler temperatures as well as varieties of vegetation that form habitats for cicadas adapted to high altitude environments.

6. Urbanization: While cicadas are primarily associated with natural habitats, some species have adapted to urban environments and can be found in parks, gardens, and green spaces within cities. Urbanization alters habitat structure and introduces new food sources, creating opportunities for cicadas to colonize urban areas and exploit human-modified landscapes.

Overall, cicadas exhibit diverse habitat preferences shaped by factors such as vegetation, moisture, temperature, soil type, altitude, and urbanization. Understanding these preferences is essential for conservation efforts and habitat management strategies aimed at preserving cicada populations and their associated ecosystems. By protecting and restoring habitats that meet the needs of cicadas, we can ensure the continued survival and ecological importance of these remarkable insects.

Chapter 4: Cicada's Behaviors

Reproduction

Cicadas have a remarkable reproductive cycle that is necessary for their life cycle and species' continuation. Several stages are involved in this process, from courtship and mating to egg-laying and nymph emergence.

1. Courtship and Mating: Using specialized structures called tymbals, male cicadas produce loud, distinctive calls which serve as mating signals to females. These calls differ in frequency and amplitude according to the species and act as a way of identifying suitable mates. Mating occurs after a female has been attracted into the canopy of trees where cicadas spend most of their adult lives.

2. Egg-Laying: After copulation, female cicadas search for places with good conditions for egg deposition. They insert the eggs they lay into cuts that they make on branches of trees, twigs or stems using ovipositors.As such,a single female can lay hundreds of eggs deposited singly in rows under bark or plant tissue so that when they hatch into nymphs;they will still be able to get nourished by the host plant's nutrients.

3. Nymph development: Other than eggs hatching into tiny naiads, there is also another phase that they go through once laid; incubation stage. These small nymphs then either fall or crawl down to the ground where they dig into the soil to start their subterranean development. The underground nymphs depend on sap from plant roots and move through several molts at different stages of a few years depending on its type.

4. Emergence: A group of young cicadas which have been developing under the earth emerge from the ground as one due to different aspects like temperature changes and moisture content in the earth. This emergence in hundreds of thousands is an incredible sight, with millions of cicadas emerging together overwhelming their predators so as to increase their chances for successful mating and reproduction.

The life cycle of cicadas has a reproductive cycle involving elaborate interconnections that guarantee survival of species. Through an understanding about various steps involved in cicada breeding, scientists can be enlightened about their ecology, behavior and population dynamics thus contributing to conservation initiatives associated with these extraordinary insects including their habitats.

Cicadas Communication

Cicadas are well-known for their outstanding and complex communication methods which play a significant role in the survival, mating as well as general behavior. Their communication is primarily through loud buzzing calls but they also use other sensory signals to communicate with each other and their habitat.

1. Acoustic Communication: The most common form of communication among cicadas is acoustic signaling. The males produce high-volume calls by using specialized organs known as tymbals situated at the sides of their abdomen. Cicadas create sounds of buzzing or clicking by vibrating these tymbals rapidly that go for far distances. Each species of cicada has its distinct call, allowing individuals to recognize and locate potential mates. These calls serve several purposes including attracting mates, establishing territories, and synchronizing mating behavior during mass emergence.

2. Cicada Acoustic Signals and Behaviors: Cicadas have various acoustic signals and behaviors that they use to communicate with each other. These include the courtship calls, made by males to attract females for mating as well as territorial calls through which males protect their territories from competitors. Males of some species sing duets where each one makes a sound then another one follows so that they can mate together or establish group hierarchy. Also, cicadas sometimes create alarm calls in response to dangers or disturbances; hence warning nearby individuals who are at risk.

3. Chemical Communication: Apart from acoustical signaling, cicadas have also adopted chemical communication as an effective channel of communicating. The male cicada therefore emits pheromones into the air when it needs to lure the female for sexual reproduction chemicals used by females to pick up this scent enabling them to land onto possible mates of the same species. At times, these pheromones are also produced by some species of cicadas in order to enable them synchronize their emergence with that of others around them and in turn allow successful reproduction during mass emergence.

4. Visual Signals: Despite being less conspicuous than acoustic and chemical communication, cicadas also use visual signals to communicate with one another. To entice females or establish their dominance over groups, male cicada may enact certain behaviors or assume specific postures. Furthermore, there are species that have wings that are brightly colored or patterned as well; this may be an indication of courtship and mating.

Cicadas make use of a combination of acoustic, chemical and visual signals for communication among themselves and synchronizing their actions. These modes of communication are essential for identifying mates, establishing territories and coordinating mating activities thus contributing towards the reproductive success and survival of cicada populations. Understanding how cicadas communicate is crucial in studying their behavior, ecology and evolutionary relationships which will provide important insights on the biology of these amazing insects.

Feeding Habits

Cicadas are well-known for their loud calls and remarkable life cycles; however, their feeding habits dominate. These species' feeding habits differ greatly from each other and also change with the age of individual insects. Knowledge about cicada feeding is important in comprehending their place in the ecosystem and influence on the environment.

1. Juvenile Cicada: During this period which may take many years, cicadas feed on xylem sap only. They penetrate into plant tissues using their sharp sucking mouthparts to reach xylem vessels in trees and shrubs and get nutritious sap out of them. Such a manner of nutrition sometimes causes harm to host plants, especially if lots of bugs come together or when there is a concurrent stress such as dryness or disease. However, they rarely have any significance to most trees' fitness and are more often perceived as pests than primary impediments to plant vitality.

2. Adult Feeding Habits: After the cicadas emerge from the ground and become adults, their major concentration shifts from feeding to reproduction. Adult cicadas have forelegs that are not adapted for chewing or biting. Instead they use them to penetrate plant tissue and access xylem or phloem sap. Nonetheless, adult cicadas rarely feed much if at all during their brief aerial life while surviving above ground because of a few weeks up to few months depending on different species. Rather they mainly survive on energy stored in the nymphal stage for breeding.

3. Potential Ecological Impacts: Cicadas may not be considered serious pests due to limited feeding as adults; however, the appearance of large numbers can bring about some ecological consequences. For example, ovipositing by mature females (egg-laying) may slightly damage small trees and shrubs when there is a mass exodus of cicadas leading to branch dieback or deformation where tender twigs have been chosen for egg deposition. In addition, dead bodies of adult male insects that accumulate after this period within forests could also help recycle nutrients across the ecosystem through feeding scavengers and decomposers alike.

4. Ecosystem Role: Despite their minor impact on the health of plants, cicadas have an important part in the dynamics of ecosystems. Thus, cicadas are food for numerous predators such as birds, mammals, reptiles and insects; hence serve as good sources of energy in food chains or webs. This can lead to population explosions of predator species with larger numbers of emergent predators thronging other insect populations leading to more predation pressure on them. In addition, nutrients that are reabsorbed from dead bodies of these insects make forest soils fertile, supporting vegetation growth and productivity of the ecosystem.

Cicadas may not cause significant damage to crops but their feeding habits and life cycles have ecological implications with regard to the environment. Therefore, it is vital to understand their place in ecosystems if we want to manage their populations and promote biodiversity conservation in areas where they are indigenous.

Chapter 5: The Role of Cicadas in Nature

Ecological Importance

Cicadas hold significant ecological importance in various ecosystems around the world, contributing to nutrient cycling, biodiversity, and ecosystem dynamics. Understanding their ecological role is essential for conserving these fascinating insects and maintaining the health of their habitats.

1. Nutrient Cycling: Cicadas play a vital role in nutrient cycling within forest ecosystems. During their underground nymphal stage, cicadas feed on the sap of tree roots, extracting nutrients from the xylem fluid. When they emerge as adults, they molt and leave behind their exoskeletons, which contain valuable nutrients. Additionally, adult cicadas die after mating and laying eggs, contributing their bodies to the forest floor. These carcasses decompose, releasing nutrients back into the soil, where they can be absorbed by plants and contribute to ecosystem productivity. The recycling of nutrients through cicada life cycles helps maintain the fertility of forest soils and supports the growth of vegetation.

2. Food Source: Cicadas serve as an essential food source for a wide range of predators, including birds, mammals, reptiles, amphibians, and insects. Their emergence in large numbers provides a temporary boon for predators, triggering population increases and promoting biodiversity within ecosystems. Many species of birds, such as woodpeckers, swallows, and warblers, rely on cicadas as a primary food source during their breeding season. Similarly, mammals like bats and rodents, as well as reptiles such as snakes and lizards, opportunistically feed on adult cicadas, helping regulate their populations and contributing to the balance of predator-prey relationships.

3. Pollination: While cicadas are not as efficient pollinators as bees or butterflies, they play a minor role in pollination by visiting flowers to feed on nectar. Although they lack specialized structures for collecting pollen, cicadas inadvertently transfer pollen between flowers as they move from plant to plant in search of food. While their contribution to pollination is relatively small compared to other insect pollinators, it still helps ensure the reproductive success of some plant species within their habitats.

4. Indicators of Ecosystem Health: Cicadas can also serve as indicators of ecosystem health and environmental conditions. Because their life cycles are closely tied to the availability of suitable habitat and climatic factors, changes in cicada populations or emergence patterns can reflect broader shifts in ecosystem dynamics. For example, alterations in land use, deforestation, or climate change can impact cicada populations by disrupting their breeding sites or altering temperature and moisture regimes. Monitoring cicada populations can provide valuable insights into the health of forest ecosystems and help guide conservation efforts to protect these habitats and the species that depend on them.

Cicadas play a multifaceted role in ecosystems as contributors to nutrient cycling, important food sources for predators, minor pollinators, and indicators of environmental health. Recognizing their ecological importance is crucial for conserving these insects and maintaining the balance of biodiversity in their habitats.

Cicadas Interactions with Other Species

Cicadas are not solitary creatures; they interact with a multitude of other species in their ecosystems, shaping ecological dynamics and contributing to the intricate web of life. These interactions span across various trophic levels and ecological processes, influencing both cicadas and the organisms they interact with.

1. Predator-Prey Interactions: One of the most prominent interactions involving cicadas is their relationship with predators. Cicada nymphs are vulnerable to predation by underground-dwelling organisms such as predatory insects, spiders, and small mammals. However, it is during the adult stage, when cicadas emerge en masse, that they become a significant food source for a diverse array of predators. Birds, including species like woodpeckers, grosbeaks, and flycatchers, are known to exploit cicada emergence, feasting on the abundant insects to fuel their breeding efforts. Mammals such as bats, rodents, and some primates also capitalize on the cicada bounty, contributing to the regulation of cicada populations and the dynamics of predator-prey relationships in their habitats.

2. Parasitism: Cicadas are not immune to parasitic interactions. Various parasitoid wasps and flies target cicadas at different stages of their life cycle, utilizing them as hosts for their developing larvae. Female parasitoids often lay their eggs on or near cicada nymphs or adults, and upon hatching, the parasitic larvae feed on the cicadas, eventually killing them. This parasitic pressure can have significant impacts on cicada populations, influencing their abundance and distribution within ecosystems.

3. Symbiotic Relationships: Cicadas also engage in symbiotic relationships with other organisms. One notable example is the relationship between cicadas and certain species of bacteria that reside in specialized organs within their bodies. These bacteria, known as endosymbionts, provide essential nutrients to cicadas and aid in their digestion of xylem sap, which forms a significant portion of their diet during the nymphal stage. In return, cicadas provide a protected environment for the bacteria to thrive and reproduce. This mutualistic association highlights the intricate dependencies that exist between organisms in natural systems.

4. Competition: Competition for resources, such as food and breeding sites, can occur among cicadas themselves and with other insect species. In areas where multiple cicada species coexist, competition for host plants and mating opportunities may influence their distribution and abundance. Similarly, competition with other herbivorous insects or with organisms that utilize similar resources underground can shape cicada populations and community dynamics.

5. Indirect Effects: Cicadas can also have indirect effects on other species and ecosystem processes. For example, their emergence in large numbers can lead to increased nutrient input into the soil through the deposition of exuviae and carcasses, influencing soil microbial communities and nutrient cycling processes. Additionally, the loud mating calls of male cicadas can attract predators, inadvertently affecting the behavior and distribution of other organisms in the vicinity.

Overall, cicadas participate in a complex web of interactions with other species, influencing ecological processes and shaping the structure and function of their ecosystems. Understanding these interactions is essential for comprehensively assessing the ecological roles of cicadas and their impacts on ecosystem dynamics.

Chapter 6: Cicadas in Culture and Folklore

Historical References

Throughout history, cicadas have captured the imagination of cultures around the world, leaving an indelible mark on literature, art, and folklore. Their distinctive sounds, remarkable life cycle, and periodic emergencies have fascinated and inspired people across different civilizations, leading to a rich tapestry of historical references spanning millennia.

1. Symbolism and Mythology: In many cultures, cicadas have been imbued with symbolic significance and mythological interpretations. In ancient Greece, cicadas were associated with immortality and resurrection due to their emergence from the ground after long periods of dormancy. Greek poets and philosophers referenced cicadas in their works, portraying them as symbols of rebirth and the soul's journey to the afterlife. Similarly, in Chinese culture, cicadas symbolize longevity, renewal, and transformation. They are often depicted in art and literature as symbols of immortality and spiritual enlightenment, with their shrill calls evoking themes of perseverance and resilience.

2. Literary References: Cicadas have also found their way into the works of numerous writers and poets throughout history. From ancient Greek epics to modern novels, cicadas have been celebrated for their evocative symbolism and unique life cycle. In Japanese literature, cicadas are a common motif, symbolizing the fleeting nature of life and the passage of time. Haiku poets frequently incorporate the sounds of cicadas into their verses, capturing the essence of summer and the ephemeral beauty of nature. In Western literature, cicadas have been featured in works ranging from Shakespearean sonnets to contemporary fiction, serving as metaphors for themes of renewal, transformation, and the cyclical nature of existence.

3. Artistic Depictions: Cicadas have inspired artists and craftsmen across cultures to create intricate representations in various art forms. From ancient pottery and sculptures to modern paintings and ceramics, cicadas have been depicted in diverse artistic styles, reflecting their cultural significance and aesthetic appeal. In ancient Mesoamerican civilizations like the Aztecs and Maya, cicadas were depicted in sculptures and jewelry, symbolizing fertility, abundance, and the cycle of life. In contemporary art, cicadas continue to inspire artists, with their striking appearance and melodious songs serving as sources of inspiration for paintings, sculptures, and mixed-media installations.

4. Folklore and Superstitions: Cicadas feature prominently in the folklore and superstitions of many cultures, often as harbingers of good or bad omens. In some African cultures, the appearance of cicadas is believed to signal the onset of rainy seasons or the presence of ancestral spirits. In ancient Rome, the chirping of cicadas was thought to foretell imminent rain or heat waves, leading to various superstitions and rituals to appease these insects. Similarly, in parts of Asia, cicadas are believed to possess supernatural powers and are revered as protectors of crops and guardians of the natural world.

5. Scientific Discovery: Beyond their cultural and artistic significance, cicadas have also played a role in scientific discovery and exploration. Early naturalists and entomologists studied cicadas to better understand their biology, behavior, and distribution, laying the groundwork for modern scientific research. Today, cicadas continue to be subjects of scientific inquiry, with researchers investigating their genetics, physiology, and ecological interactions to gain insights into broader evolutionary and ecological processes.

Cicadas hold a prominent place in human history and culture, serving as symbols of resilience, renewal, and the interconnectedness of life. From ancient myths and literary classics to contemporary art and scientific inquiry, cicadas continue to captivate and inspire people across the globe, leaving a legacy that transcends time and geography.

Cultural Significances

Cicadas hold a profound cultural significance in various societies around the world, symbolizing themes of rebirth, immortality, and the cyclical nature of life. Their distinctive calls, seasonal emergence, and remarkable life cycle have inspired myths, rituals, and artistic expressions across different cultures, shaping collective beliefs and traditions for centuries.

1. Symbol of Resilience: In many cultures, cicadas symbolize resilience and endurance in the face of adversity. Their ability to survive long periods underground before emerging into the sunlight mirrors the human experience of overcoming challenges and hardships. In ancient Greek mythology, cicadas were associated with the story of Tithonus, a mortal who was transformed into a cicada by the gods, symbolizing the immortal soul's journey through life and death. Similarly, in Japanese culture, cicadas are admired for their perseverance and tenacity, echoing the spirit of resilience in the face of adversity.

2. Harbingers of Summer: The buzzing chorus of cicadas heralds the arrival of summer in many parts of the world, marking a seasonal transition and evoking a sense of nostalgia and anticipation. In Japan, the sound of cicadas, known as "semi" in Japanese, is synonymous with the sweltering heat of summer and the vibrant energy of the season. Cicada-themed festivals and celebrations are held across Japan to commemorate their emergence, featuring traditional rituals, folk songs, and culinary delights inspired by these iconic insects.

3. Spiritual Symbols: Cicadas are often imbued with spiritual significance in various religious and cultural traditions, representing themes of transformation, renewal, and spiritual enlightenment. In ancient China, cicadas were revered as symbols of immortality and reincarnation, with their periodic emergence symbolizing the cycle of life, death, and rebirth. Cicada motifs frequently appear in Chinese art, literature, and folklore, reflecting their enduring spiritual symbolism and cultural significance.

4. Artistic Inspiration: Cicadas have inspired artists, poets, and craftsmen across cultures to create intricate representations in various art forms. From ancient sculptures and paintings to modern literature and music, cicadas have been celebrated for their aesthetic beauty and symbolic resonance. In ancient Egypt, cicadas were depicted in hieroglyphics and tomb paintings, symbolizing fertility, abundance, and the eternal cycle of life. In contemporary art, cicadas continue to inspire artists, with their striking appearance and melodious songs serving as sources of creative inspiration and artistic expression.

5. Folklore and Superstitions: Cicadas feature prominently in the folklore and superstitions of many cultures, often as omens of good or bad fortune. In some African cultures, the appearance of cicadas is believed to signal the presence of ancestral spirits or the beginning of a new agricultural season. In ancient Rome, the chirping of cicadas was thought to foretell imminent rain or drought, leading to various superstitions and rituals to appease these insects. Similarly, in parts of Asia, cicadas are associated with supernatural powers and are believed to bring blessings or curses depending on their behavior and appearance.

Cicadas occupy a unique place in human culture, serving as symbols of resilience, renewal, and spiritual significance across different civilizations. From ancient myths and rituals to contemporary art and folklore, cicadas continue to inspire awe and fascination, connecting people to the rhythms of nature and the mysteries of the cosmos. Their cultural significance transcends geographical boundaries and temporal divides, uniting humanity in a shared reverence for these enigmatic insects and the timeless wisdom they embody.

Conclusion

Cicadas, like many other organisms, face a variety of threats that can impact their populations and overall health. These threats range from habitat loss and climate change to human activities and invasive species, all of which can have significant implications for cicada populations and their ecological roles.

1. Habitat Loss and Fragmentation: One of the most significant threats to cicada populations is habitat loss and fragmentation due to urbanization, agriculture, and land development.

Cicadas require specific habitats for feeding, mating, and egg-laying, and the destruction or alteration of these habitats can disrupt their life cycle and reproductive success. Fragmentation of habitat also isolates cicada populations, making them more vulnerable to genetic isolation and local extinction.

2. Climate Change: Climate change poses a serious threat to cicada populations by altering temperature and precipitation patterns, which can disrupt their emergence and mating behaviors. Rising temperatures may trigger premature emergences or delay cicada emergences, reducing their synchrony and impacting population dynamics. Changes in precipitation patterns can also affect soil moisture levels, which may influence cicada egg-laying and nymph survival. Additionally, climate change can alter the distribution of cicada species, leading to shifts in their geographic range and interactions with other species.

3. Pesticide Use: The widespread use of pesticides in agriculture and landscaping can have detrimental effects on cicada populations by directly poisoning adult cicadas and nymphs or indirectly impacting their food sources and habitat quality. Insecticides used to control pest insects may inadvertently harm non-target species, including cicadas, by reducing their abundance and reproductive success. Furthermore, pesticides can accumulate in the environment, contaminating soil, water, and vegetation, and affecting the entire ecosystem.

4. Invasive Species: Invasive species pose a threat to native cicada populations by competing for resources, preying on cicada nymphs, or disrupting their natural habitat. For example, invasive plants can outcompete native vegetation, reducing the availability of suitable food sources for cicadas. Invasive predators, such as birds, mammals, and predatory insects, may consume cicada nymphs or adults, reducing their population size and reproductive output. Additionally, invasive pathogens and parasites can infect cicadas, weakening their immune systems and increasing their susceptibility to disease.

5. Human Disturbance: Human activities, such as deforestation, pollution, and recreational activities, can disturb cicada habitats and disrupt their life cycle. Deforestation removes essential habitat for cicadas, while pollution from industrial and agricultural sources can degrade water quality and soil health, affecting cicada nymphs and their food sources. Recreational activities, such as off-road vehicle use and hiking, can trample cicada eggs and nymphs and disturb adult cicadas during mating and oviposition.

Cicadas face a variety of threats to their populations, ranging from habitat loss and climate change to pesticide use and invasive species. Addressing these threats requires coordinated conservation efforts aimed at protecting and restoring cicada habitats, reducing pesticide use, controlling invasive species, and mitigating the impacts of human disturbance on cicada populations. By understanding the factors contributing to cicada declines and implementing effective conservation strategies, we can help ensure the long-term survival of these fascinating insects and their important ecological roles.